PET LOSS GRIEF JOURNAL: 3 MINUTES A DAY

30 Days of Guided Reflection and Healing Prompts for Grieving Pet Owners

KATIE KUPERMAN

Copyright © 2025 Katie Kuperman

Published by Striking Content Inc.

All rights reserved. No part of this book may be reproduced, stored in a retrieval system, or transmitted in any form or by any means—electronic, mechanical, photocopying, recording, or otherwise—without the prior written permission of the publisher, except for brief quotations used in reviews, articles, or scholarly works.

This journal is intended as a supportive resource to help navigate the grief and healing process after the loss of a beloved pet. It is not a substitute for professional mental health services.

For permissions or inquiries, please contact: katie@katiekuperman.com.

Printed in USA.

ISBN Print: 978-1-0691701-2-5

ISBN eBook: 978-1-0691701-3-2

To all the incredible pets who have come and gone.

CONTENTS

A FRIENDLY WARNING & DISCLAIMER — vii
INTRODUCTION — viii

DAY 1 — 1
Saying Goodbye

DAY 2 — 6
Aching Heart

DAY 3 — 10
Shock

DAY 4 — 14
Reluctance

DAY 5 — 18
Cherishing the Memories

DAY 6 — 22
It Comes in Waves

DAY 7 — 26
Setback

DAY 8 — 30
Anger

DAY 9 — 34
Keeping Busy

DAY 10 — 38
Easing Your Pain

DAY 11 — 42
Guilt

DAY 12 — 46
Smile Again

DAY 13 — 50
Regrets & Unspoken Words

DAY 14 — 54
Unique Personality

DAY 15 — 58
The Hardest Part

DAY 16 — 62
Coping with Loneliness

DAY 17   66
Signs and Symbols

DAY 18   70
What Your Pet Taught You

DAY 19   74
Shifting Focus

DAY 20   78
Adapting

DAY 21   82
Progress

DAY 22   86
The Day We Met

DAY 23   90
Dreaming of Them

DAY 24   94
A Tribute to Your Pet's Life

DAY 25   98
Finding Comfort

DAY 26   102
The Love that Remains

DAY 27   106
Warming Up to the Idea of Another

DAY 28   110
Forever in Your Heart

DAY 29   114
Finding Peace

DAY 30   118
Being Happy

THANK YOU   123

A FRIENDLY WARNING & DISCLAIMER

Friendly warning

This book necessarily deals with an emotional and possibly traumatic event that you've experienced. Please participate at your own discretion.

Disclaimer

This book reflects my personal experience and research in pet loss and the grieving process. Please note that I am not a therapist. If you are in deep distress or severely struggling, be sure to seek professional help.

INTRODUCTION

My idea to create this book and journal comes from personal life experience. I lost one of the great loves in my life: my cat, Hank. While I knew it was going to be a huge loss to mourn, it's been even harder than I anticipated. I needed a plan and a process for my mourning – something a little extra.

I thought to myself: *what better way to work through my own impossible pain and grief over the loss of Hank than to create a journal that I can use?* And then that morphed into: *I'll publish it and maybe others can benefit from it, too.*

So, here I am.

This journal is unique in the sense that it's a reflection of my personal experience. Each day represents my own strong sentiment on that particular day in the cycle. There are writings, quotes and guided journaling prompts each day that reflect precisely what I felt I needed and was ready for at that point in

INTRODUCTION

time, as I progressed through the grief process. Every word of this journal comes from a real place, because I lived and breathed all of it right in the moment. I was once in the same boat you find yourself in right now.

The order of your feelings and experiences may not be the same as mine, so if you think it's necessary, I invite you to flip through this book and find the way you feel on any given day. Your Day 2 might be my Day 10, and your Day 12 might be my Day 3. The order of emotions isn't what's important. How we face, process and deal with these emotions is what matters. Writing this book and journal has been a huge help in my own personal healing process.

The act of self-reflection is incredibly powerful as you deal with what feels like the impossible. The second piece is writing. For centuries, writing has been known to be a therapeutic activity, through which we can feel a release and a sense of peace. Take a minute (or five) each day to explore this book and to journal about what you're feeling. I promise, each day that you do this, you'll feel better when you're done.

As you move through this book, you'll notice I don't delve into Elisabeth Kübler-Ross' Five Stages of Grief (denial, anger, bargaining, depression and acceptance), nor do I go into the specifics of J. William Worden's Four Tasks of Mourning (1-accepting the reality of the loss; 2-processing the pain of grief; 3-adjusting to a world without the deceased; 4-finding a way to remember the deceased while continuing life) or Margaret Stroebe and Henk Schut's Dual Process Model of Grief (loss-oriented coping and restoration-oriented coping). This is deliberate because everyone experiences loss differently. All experi-

INTRODUCTION

ences are right and there's no such thing as a wrong path or a missed step. Having said that, you're bound to find overlaps and touchpoints that relate to the different stages of grief as well as the inevitable tasks associated with mourning. It is my intention that you find comfort in knowing you're not alone and that whatever you're feeling is okay. There are hard truths you'll need to face but there's always a silver lining that illuminates effective ways to deal with those, helping you form a new path where joy co-exists with your grief.

One thing I find particularly helpful throughout my grieving process is talking to others in my life who know precisely what it's like to lose a pet. As you work through this journal with me, I want you to know that I get it. I understand what you're going through and even if it feels like others around you don't, there are plenty of us who do. And we're in it together.

I believe the bond between pets and humans is profoundly special. Without language to bind us, we find other ways to connect. Through eye contact, touch and daily care, there forms a deep trust, an understanding of one another, a special bond that envelopes our love tightly. It's an intuitive connection that runs far deeper than words.

Following the ordeal my husband and I shared with a tyrant cat of the Jekyll and Hyde type, came our savior, Hank. Through the glass window of the shelter that day, we chose each other. And he couldn't have been more different from what we were accustomed to – a kind, gentle, loving feline soul who swept us off our feet. For the next decade, we shared our lives, closely knit together. From me, to my husband, to my two children, every one of us fostered and nurtured an incredible bond with him. He

INTRODUCTION

filled our lives with love, laughter, fluffy snuggles and the loudest purr you've ever heard. There were tough times, though. He was a cat with nine lives, battling inflammatory bowel disease (**IBD**), a urinary tract blockage, gingivitis and several "accidental" escapes from our house. We survived it all. Finally, oral cancer took him from us. For the last seven months of his life, there was a slow deterioration, from losing his hearing, to **IBD** flareups, to thyroid elevations, and finally, a metastasized malignant tumor under the tongue that stopped him from eating, no matter how much he still wanted to.

It was excruciatingly difficult to watch him suffer in the last week of his life. Regardless of how he maintained his sweet and lovable demeanor, never failing to purr the moment you came to pet him, I knew how much he was struggling. I also knew the end of his life was near. The night before the call from the doctor, as I watched him battle to swallow even his most beloved Temptations treats, it hit me like a ton of bricks. I began to weep on my kitchen floor where we sat together. I embraced him with all my love and told him I was there for him.

Still, when the call came on Sunday and we had to *accept* our new reality, my heart began to ache and I felt like I was going to vomit. That feeling didn't go away for days.

The four of us spent the whole day with our feline boy, snuggling him, helping him eat even the tiniest of sprinkles of food and keeping him comfortable. In the afternoon, it was time. We couldn't let him suffer any longer and the anticipation for what was coming was too much to bear. It got to the point where we made an important realization: we were keeping him here for us, not him. That's a hard reality to accept.

INTRODUCTION

An hour later, he died in our arms.

I believe human beings who are pet owners have an added layer of selflessness. We choose to care for an animal and never question what that entails. In return, we have unwavering companionship. The score is never tallied and there are no petty calculations of gives and takes. On the contrary, a beautiful understanding forms between us, forever to be honored. We let ourselves be vulnerable and open our hearts to pure, unconditional love. While it lasts, it's one of the greatest experiences of our lives. But when it ends, the blow comes hard and fast. We chose to love big, and now we have no choice but to grieve big too.

So, let's get on with it.

We can do this.

DAY 1
SAYING GOODBYE

The hard truth

This is the hardest.

Without question, pain and suffering are at an all-time high on this day. Not only for you, but also for your companion pet. Whether the end comes fast or slow, all of a sudden or in the form of a gradual buildup, the final 24 hours mark the day when your pet is at their worst, and as a result, so are you.

You knew this day would come, and yet every part of your being wished it wouldn't. For years, it's been the day that was far too difficult even to think about. If ever the fear of losing your companion flashed into your mind, you'd quickly shake it away because the mere thought was unbearable.

And now?

It's here. The day has come. You're not ready. But then again, you never would have been. Even if you had a feeling, even if your intuition told you the end was near, the actual moment when it all becomes real seems impossible. Untrue. Some kind of nightmare you're going to wake up from.

When the terrible news arrives, you may scream, cry, crumble to the ground. It feels as though you can't do it, you can't live it, you can't get through it, and yet you know all too well that you have to. There's no choice and this has become your living reality.

If your companion passes suddenly, shock sets in. You won't believe it. Robbed of any time to comprehend or process what's happening, you're bewildered and beside yourself. In this case, it takes more time for you to come to terms with your loss.

On the other hand, if your pet has been deteriorating for some time, is sick or terminally ill and euthanasia is the clear but oh-so-difficult answer, your grieving process begins from the moment that awful word is uttered to you by the vet. I despise that word – not only because it's one of the hardest things you'll ever have to do, but also because I can't help but notice the contradiction of sound versus meaning. "Euth" is pronounced "youth" and yet there is nothing youthful about the procedure. Quite the opposite.

The silver lining

Take small comfort in the fact that this is the worst part. Even if the increments in your healing progress are small from here, there's only one way to go: up.

However your goodbye happens, it will feel out of this world. After the moment has come and gone, you'll wonder how you ever got through it in the first place. And then you'll realize you're tougher than you think.

"There are no goodbyes for us.
Wherever you are, you will
always be in my heart."

MAHATMA GANDHI

JOURNALING TIME

Write about the way you felt when you had to say goodbye to your companion. Let the words flow uninhibited. It doesn't need to look pretty or sound nice. It's about getting all those painful images and feelings out of your head and onto your paper.

This is a cathartic process. You'll understand what I'm talking about when you're finished.

_____
_____
_____
_____
_____
_____
_____
_____
_____
_____
_____
_____
_____
_____
_____

DAY 2
ACHING HEART

The hard truth

Without a doubt, the day you say goodbye to your pet is the absolute hardest. But be prepared for Day 2 to be an unexpected close second – or even just as hard as yesterday.

Why? Because this is the day you begin life without your pet. The usual morning routine with your companion is fresh in your mind and the heartache starts immediately, that is, if you even slept in the first place.

I woke up more times than I can count that first night after saying goodbye to my cat. Each time, for a split second I thought the pit in my stomach could have been from a bad dream until I quickly realized it wasn't. Then I tossed and turned until I caught a few more winks, which inevitably didn't last long and I found myself awake once more.

In the morning, none of us wanted to move. There were no words. Just sad faces and uncontrollable tears.

You won't want to do anything. If you can take a day off, do it. You need time to just be and to get yourself in order a little bit. Emotions are difficult to keep at bay on this day so, if at all possible, put yourself in situations that enable free expression. Holding in and bottling up are not ideal.

The silver lining

Give yourself a break. Feel all the feels.

Your goal for this day: get through it. That's all.

Reaching out to family and close friends is a great idea, particularly those who have been through this before and understand what you're feeling.

"I wanted to spend the rest of my life with you; but instead I am deeply honored knowing you spent the rest of your life with me."

CAMILLE MARCOTTE

JOURNALING TIME

Onto the lines below, unload all the things you wish you could do with your lost pet today. As painful as it will be to write this down, it will do two things:

1. You'll reflect on the rituals that became a daily routine with your companion.
2. You'll release your impossible wants and wishes onto this paper, lifting at least part of the heavy weight you now carry on your shoulders.

_____
_____
_____
_____
_____
_____
_____
_____
_____
_____
_____

DAY 3
SHOCK

The hard truth

You're shocked and in a state of disbelief.

How did I get here? Just two days ago, my companion and I were together. We went for a walk. She was on my lap. He was lying on the sofa right there beside me.

Denial is normal and an expected part of your grieving process. When you're used to something, it becomes ingrained in your daily life. We are routine-based creatures who thrive on predictability and comfort. If there's a disruption to that routine and our sense of comfort gets rattled, naturally we go through a phase where we simply can't believe it.

On this day in my own grief cycle, my son said it so well:

"Mom, I keep wishing that I'm in some kind of horrible nightmare and that

I'm going to wake up and it will all have been just a bad dream…and Hanky will still be here."

Think of a time when you've had a bad dream and then woken up in a state of anxiousness and fear. After a few seconds, in your sleepy state, you realize it was just a dream. You let out a huge sigh of relief and fall back to sleep.

This is not that. It's the opposite.

The silver lining

The only way to deal with your state of shock is to come face to face with it. You may find it comes and goes, or you might have a linear spell of disbelief before you move on to the next phase. Gently remind yourself of your reality and understand that shock and denial represent your movement through the grieving process. It's common and it's okay. Call it what it is. Talk about it. Cry about it. Journal about it.

"Denial helps us to pace our feelings of grief. There is a grace in denial. It is nature's way of letting in only as much as we can handle."

ELISABETH KÜBLER-ROSS & DAVID KESSLER

JOURNALING TIME

Is it possible you're in denial? If so, do you believe this is easing your pain in any way?

_____
_____
_____
_____
_____
_____
_____

When your brain snaps you out of it and tells you what's real, describe the physical and emotional feelings associated with that shocking moment of realization.

_____
_____
_____
_____
_____
_____
_____

DAY 4
RELUCTANCE

The hard truth

Nope. I can't. I don't want to.

Does this sum up how you're feeling today?

On this day, I found my daughter lying on her cat pillow in her room, looking sad as can be. When I walked in to hug her and ask if she was alright, she said:

"I'm not okay, Mom. And I'm not going to be okay because I don't have my Hanky."

This is the day of reluctance. The day you feel as though things ought to be better, but they're not. You understand the need to move forward, but every moment is incredibly tough. Reminders are everywhere. Plus, you've already had your life on pause for the last three days (and possibly more), caring for your pet, being there for them and giving them all the love in the world before they leave you.

You're exhausted, emotionally and physically. Death takes a toll on the living, too. All the times in your life when you've found yourself down and out, such as an argument with a loved one, a pitfall at work, a surgery, an illness or the death of someone else in your close circle, there was one place you always went: to your pet. They gave you the unconditional comfort you needed most in those moments. Without them here now, your day feels impossible to get through.

The silver lining

This is temporary. During this day (or days) of reluctance, show yourself grace. Clear your schedule, if you can. Cancel the dinner date, move the business call, catch up on the deadline tomorrow.

Do the basics. Get out of bed. Brush your teeth. Wash your face. Feed the family breakfast. Get your kids to school. This is good enough.

"Grief is a constant tug of war between trying to move forward and not wanting to at all."

HELLO TO HEAVEN

JOURNALING TIME

List all the things you DON'T want to do today (tiny or huge, list them all).

_____
_____
_____
_____
_____

Now, make a list of all the things you DID do (think small and big).

_____
_____
_____
_____
_____

See how incredible you are? There are things you couldn't do, but there are also things you *did* you. Be proud. Too often, we fail to give ourselves enough credit.

DAY 5
CHERISHING THE MEMORIES

The hard truth

Painful? Yes.

Beautiful? Yes!

Particularly if your companion was with you for some time, chances are you have boatloads of photos – and the heart-warming stories to go along with them.

Share your pet's life stories with your family and friends. Recall the day you got them, the time they peed on the kitchen floor, cute things they used to do when they were little, the way they'd sleep all curled up in a ball, or how they always knew when you needed them the most.

In my case, it was my children who started it. I didn't think I could go there; I didn't think I could do it. All those photos…all those memories. It started with them printing photos the day he left us so they could create shrines on their bulletin boards. Days later, they wanted to go back through my phone to see all kinds of early photos of him with them when they were little. Then it was changing the backgrounds on their iPads. I got drawn into the ritual.

Like I did years ago, when a previous feline treasure passed away, I created a tribute. This time it was a video with a collage of photos and loving statements. All of this made me cry all over again, but it was also a beneficial practice. It made me remember little things that I'd forgotten and it opened a well of gratitude for all the beautiful years we had together.

The silver lining

It may seem like a daunting and an almost masochistic practice, but taking a walk down memory lane turns out to be anything but. Be prepared for tears and a little more pain, but also be ready to open your heart to re-experience all the special moments you shared. At some point, it will hit you: *you're fortunate to have had your pet and they're fortunate to have had you.*

"No amount of time can erase the memory of a good cat, and no amount of masking tape can ever totally remove the fur from your couch."

LEO DWORKEN

JOURNALING TIME

What are some of your most cherished pet memories that you'll always hold dear to your heart?

_____
_____
_____
_____

Describe a few of the top photos that take the cake.

_____
_____
_____
_____
_____
_____
_____

After sharing pet stories and going back through old photos, do you feel better? Why or why not?

_____
_____
_____
_____
_____

DAY 6

IT COMES IN WAVES

The hard truth

One minute you're fine, the next you're not.

You might be cooking dinner, feeling okay and just about to put everything on a plate when the sadness overwhelms you. Or perhaps you're working and you've managed to get into a nice flow for a few hours, until you get up for a quick break and your loss slaps you in the face like a harsh winter wind. Or maybe you and your family play a game only instead of enjoying it, all you can do is think about how your pet used to be right smack in the middle of it, every time.

These are the waves. There are highs and lows. The wave forms and sails you upwards, where you manage to stay for a little while. But it only lasts so long and eventually you come crashing down with a big splash. Each time you go up, you hope it will be for an extended period of time before the inevitable downward motion comes again.

Be mindful of your triggers. Is it a time of day? A daily routine? A spot in your home? A particular smell or object?

Waves can be frustrating because it can feel as though you're moving backwards, not forwards. Rest assured, each time your wave goes up and down it's progressing closer and closer to the warmth of the shore.

The silver lining

It's bound to happen and you won't be able to stop it. There will be ups…and there will be downs. Each time your wave travels downward, try saying a hello to your pet. Utter a sweet "I love you" or "I miss you." Imagine you're giving them a huge hug.

This helps you acknowledge what you're feeling; it encourages you to sit with it for a minute and then prompts you to let it go.

"Grief is like the ocean; it comes on waves ebbing and flowing. Sometimes the water is calm, and sometimes it is overwhelming. All we can do is learn to swim."

VICKI HARRISON

 # JOURNALING TIME

Have you had a wave yet? How did it happen?

_____
_____
_____
_____

What triggers have you identified? (Think of times of day, routines, places, smells and objects.)

_____
_____
_____
_____
_____
_____

What do you do (or what would you like to do) each time your wave crashes down? How do you think this will help?

_____
_____
_____
_____
_____

DAY 7
SETBACK

The hard truth

You're going to have one. Maybe many. It comes in the form of a heaviness overtop of you. A storm cloud above your head. The lenses through which you see your world are dull and grey. Choking back tears and trying to focus on the positives of the day, it becomes clear that the outburst is inevitable. You need to cry and it needs to be *now*.

My setback came when I least expected it on this day. It had been a week and although the days were still difficult, Day 5 and Day 6 had at least felt incrementally better. Day 7 was a wallop to the stomach, sending me right back to Day 1 and Day 2 vibes. I always wake up joyful on the weekends, but not this Saturday. It felt awful. I wanted to let it all out in the kitchen, but I also didn't want to send my children right back into a painful sadness cycle. So, I held it in like any good mother would. But I also knew I couldn't do it for long.

After I prepped breakfast and did my part, I told my family I was going to work for a bit. I locked myself in my office upstairs, pulled out a picture of my cat that the kids had printed and bawled my eyes out. Telling him how I felt and thanking him for everything that he was in our lives for a decade, my tears flowed uncontrollably for a few minutes. Then I sat down at my computer and began writing the very words you're reading now. And it helped.

The silver lining

If you're having a setback, know that I'm right there with you. It's okay. Don't fight it, or it will simply bottle up and cause more pain and suffering until you let it out. Just find your safe place and grieve. Again.

Consider a small ritual with your long-lost companion. Talk to them, print a photo, draw a picture that represents how you're feeling, or journal about it right here. When you're finished, do something. Find a happy task or outing. Be around the people you love and move along with your day…just a little.

"Grieve and mourn for yourself, not once or twice, but again and again."

MORRIE SCHWARTZ

JOURNALING TIME

Write about your own setback(s). When did it come? How did it visit you? What did it feel like? How did you get through it?

_____
_____
_____
_____
_____
_____
_____
_____
_____
_____
_____
_____
_____

DAY 8
ANGER

The hard truth

Your blood is boiling today, like hot molten lava inside your body. You feel ready to erupt! The interesting part about anger during the grieving process is that its root cause isn't always clear. It's likely that you're not thinking of your lost pet at every moment as your anger simmers. The anger is there but you don't quite know why, just yet.

Your partner sets you off in the morning. You've got a short fuse with your kids. And your colleague can't seem to do anything right today. Patience seems to have run dry and happiness is nowhere to be found.

At some point throughout the day, it hits you. What you thought was just a rotten mood reveals itself as anger for your pet's loss.

Why did she have to die? Why did he have to leave me? Why was it my pet's turn to go? I hate that this is happening and I'm tired of feeling so sad!

The silver lining

Now that you've identified the reason behind your anger, it's easier to manage. Avoid certain people on this day; use your internal dialogue wisely before you speak. Tread lightly around your family members and friends. Tell people what's going on with you so they can understand and cut you some much needed slack.

Sit with your anger and let it be. This isn't about mastering your emotions but rather *feeling* them. Be comforted by the fact that it will pass soon.

"Well, everyone can master a grief but he that has it."

WILLIAM SHAKESPEARE

JOURNALING TIME

What does your anger feel like? Describe it.

_____
_____
_____
_____

Write down every question plaguing your mind today. (No matter how silly they might seem.)

_____
_____
_____
_____

At what point did you realize the source of your anger? How did you feel when you discovered why you feel so intensely angry today?

_____
_____
_____
_____

DAY 9
KEEPING BUSY

The hard truth

If you don't have something to do, chances are you'll slip right back into sadness and wallowing. The wound is too fresh and your loss is too recent for you to be completely unstimulated for extended periods of time *without* thinking about your pet.

The best thing you can do for yourself and your family right now is keep busy. Go grocery shopping. Run errands. Get to work. Finish that project you've been putting off. Cook a new and exciting dish for dinner. Bake muffins. Read a book. Take a vacation or get away for the weekend. Think of a fun activity to do with your kids. Have a date with your partner. Grab a coffee with a friend or visit your parents.

We all love our homes, but this is the place that will remind us the most of our lost companion. Here's where all the memories come flooding back into our minds and we feel the physical pain of missing our pet. Whatever you can do to get out of the house a little bit, do it. Just the simple act of being in the world and seeing others can work wonders on your state of mind and general well-being.

If you feel as though you're not ready for certain things, try doing something you've been putting off for a while, such as cleaning your closet or organizing a kitchen cupboard. It's not about running away from your feelings or your grief, but it *is* about finding a healthy balance. Grieving is okay, but maintaining good mental health is imperative.

The silver lining

As you meet up with friends, spend time with family and keep yourself occupied with work and other duties, notice the way you feel *after* any one of these activities. As opposed to the tear-filled confines of your bedroom, a healthy outing or completed project will give you a fresh perspective and make you feel a little more like your old self again.

"I keep myself busy with things to do. But every time I pause, I still think of you."

UNKNOWN SOURCE

JOURNALING TIME

List a few things you can book in over the next few days to keep you busy.

_____
_____
_____
_____
_____
_____

Think of a few tasks you've been putting off lately. Now may be the perfect time to knock those off your backend to-do list.

_____
_____
_____
_____
_____
_____

DAY 10
EASING YOUR PAIN

The hard truth

It's not good to be in a state of sorrow and suffering for an extended amount of time. Psychologists call this *prolonged grief disorder* or *dysfunctional bereavement*. This is when your painful emotions last so long and are so severe that you have trouble recovering from your loss and resuming your regular life.

The thing about grief, however, is that sometimes you want to sit in it. You want the pain to wash over your body like a hot shower. In a way, you *need* to feel the hurt. Even though it can feel like a torturous practice, experiencing the pain is essential to your healing.

At the same time, finding your balance is key. Tell yourself that it's highly likely you won't be "over" your pet for a long time now. Once you acknowledge this, then the most logical next step becomes clear: you need to find a way to live *with* grief. True love never dies and neither does your grieving process. Instead of waiting for it to pass, figure out ways to ease your pain, find joy and live with your loss.

The silver lining

Suffering is inevitable but it doesn't need to define your existence. Feel the pain and experience the sorrow, but don't let it take you over. In time, what you'll find is that you still have moments and the sadness hasn't disappeared, but what you also have is your life and all the greatness that comes along with it.

"The risk of love is loss, and the price of loss is grief. But the pain of grief is only a shadow when compared with the pain of never risking love."

HILARY STANTON ZUNIN

JOURNALING TIME

Write about your favorite place to grieve. Where do you go to let it all out?

_____
_____
_____
_____
_____
_____

Write down a few ways you can ease your pain and make a point of carving out time for these activities or practices in the days and weeks ahead.

_____
_____
_____
_____
_____
_____

DAY 11
GUILT

The hard truth

You may feel a sense of guilt associated with your pet's loss. Maybe you feel bad about having fun without them, especially with a surviving pet. Perhaps you wish you snuggled them more when they were still here. Maybe you're haunted by the way you handled the last few days they had. Or you may feel guilty about making that inconceivably hard decision to end your pet's life and stop their suffering, when they didn't know what was happening and you couldn't explain it to them.

Block out any attempts to invalidate your feelings – whether they're coming from you or other people. Intrusive thoughts may seep into your mind. Don't fall into the judgmental, cultural trap of "it was just an animal and not a human being." It doesn't matter. Your pet was a member of your family and a big part of your life. This loss is just as profound as any other.

Refrain from making comparisons and passing judgments. They are meaningless. There is no reason to feel guilty about how upset you are or about the past you cannot change. Whatever we choose to love in our lives, if we really open our hearts and create a deeply meaningful relationship, the loss is extremely difficult to navigate, irrespective of who or what it was.

Guilt is part of grief. When we're stricken by a painful loss, it's in our nature to to feel guilty about the things we did or didn't do.

The silver lining

Your pet doesn't feel guilty, sad or lonely about leaving you. Now that they're on the other side of the Rainbow Bridge (scan the QR code at the end of this journal to find out what this special place is), they have an understanding that you cannot see with full clarity just yet. They know it was their time and they feel joy to have shared all the days they had here on Earth with *you*, the person who *did* do enough and who was *everything* they needed you to be.

It's time for you to embrace the same sentiment.

"Here's the thing: every loss is valid. And every loss is not the same. You can't flatten the landscape of grief and say that everything is equal. It isn't."

MEGAN DEVINE

JOURNALING TIME

Do you feel guilty about your pet's loss? Why or why not?

_____
_____
_____

Do you have any regrets? Describe them.

_____
_____
_____

If your pet could talk, what do you think they would want you to know right now?

_____
_____
_____

DAY 12
SMILE AGAIN

The hard truth

Just because you're smiling, doesn't mean you're not grieving. The two co-exist and they will for quite some time. Think of your smile and your grief holding hands, moving through life together in some mysterious form of harmony.

Today is about celebrating the smile upon your face. Whether your smile finds its way back on Day 2 or Day 20, feel good about it being there. Don't think twice and don't let it appear with a side of guilt. Let it be, enjoy the feeling and remember that it's okay to smile and feel happy again - your pet wants this for you.

The simple act of smiling is an excellent form of coping. A little smile can ease the pain of your grief and serve as a reminder that there's still so much to be happy about and grateful for. The more smiles that come, the more you'll realize there is more to life, if only you begin to let it in.

The silver lining

Whenever your smile first starts to reappear, be comforted by it. Know that it will start to make its appearance more and more. Enjoy it and don't feel bad about it. Pay attention to which people, things and activities bring out your smile and surround yourself with them more often.

"Smile at the memory of your beautiful pet, for they lit up this world with their joyous spirit."

UNKNOWN SOURCE

JOURNALING TIME

When did you first notice your smile come back? What were you doing?

_____
_____
_____
_____
_____

What in your life regularly makes you smile? Make a weekly plan to plug in more of these things.

_____
_____
_____
_____
_____

DAY 13
REGRETS & UNSPOKEN WORDS

The hard truth

I often talk about the power of the human-pet relationship that exists without words. Sure, you talk to your pet (maybe still, even though they're gone – I know I do) and they bark, meow, sing or squeak back to you. But it isn't the same speech and word-based form of communication human beings share between one another.

The communication between you and your pet has no words; it runs far deeper. We find unspoken ways to connect with one another through the years. And we explore different methods of care, discipline, company and affection.

Now that your pet is gone, you'll likely find yourself walking down the Road of Regrets at some point. What didn't you do? What did you do that you wish you hadn't? Did you spend enough time? Did you give enough snuggles? Did they know how much you loved them?

Regret is a part of grief. Our minds are often plagued by regretful thoughts as we struggle to cope with the fact that our time is up.

There's no way to fix anything or bring them back. We aren't gifted with do-overs in this life. If you find yourself thinking of many words you wished you'd whispered to them or things you wish you did, tell them now.

The silver lining

Talk to your pet. Tell them what's on your mind. Speak to them anytime. Why not? Release those thoughts and feelings. They're listening.

Know in your heart that what you gave was enough – more than enough. If you're grieving now, this means you shared an unbreakable bond with your pet while they were here. Understand that the Road of Regrets is nothing more than a street we all walk down after a loss. Just because it's inevitable, doesn't mean it's real.

"What we once enjoyed and deeply loved we can never lose, for all that we love deeply becomes part of us."

HELEN KELLER

JOURNALING TIME

Write down all the unspoken words you want to say to your pet.

_____
_____
_____
_____
_____

Write down your regrets (however true or false they may be) now that your pet is gone.

_____
_____
_____
_____
_____

DAY 14
UNIQUE PERSONALITY

The hard truth

One of the most difficult parts of losing someone is coming to terms with the fact that we are all unique individuals. No two humans are the same; no two animals are the same. You'll never again enjoy the quirks and distinctive habits of your pet. Any other pet you choose to own will have a whole new set of characteristics, but they'll never be the same.

Betty, the first cat I lost as an adult woman, had the sweetest and most chipper personality. She was always "talking to me," her cute little meow ringing through our home as she followed me around. My most recent loss, Hank, was a one-of-a-kind character, to say the least. He had an on-command purr as loud as a motorboat, the willingness to be picked up and snuggled at all times of day, a gentle soul and the hilarious habit of "catching" little stuffies and rolled up socks (which I can only assume were his versions of indoor mice) and bringing them to us, all the while howling as though he were possessed.

When I think of these special traits, it makes my heart ache all over again, knowing I'll never hear Betty's voice or Hank's purr ever again. What helps, though, is telling stories. Sharing. Remembering. By doing this, we ensure that their unique personality traits live on.

The silver lining

Even though you'll never be able to replicate the things that made your pet so irreplaceably perfect, there are lots of other animal traits out there that are beautiful in their own right. Maybe you'll experience other special personalities down the road. When you're ready, of course.

"Animal sentience has been proven many times over, meaning that, like humans, they have unique personalities, feel pain, and have an intrinsic will to live."

BENJAHMIN KOENIGSBERG

 # JOURNALING TIME

Write down all the unique personality traits that made your pet one of a kind. Instead of feeling sad about their absence, celebrate the fact that you got to experience and love each and every one of those individual characteristics (even the annoying ones).

_____
_____
_____
_____
_____
_____
_____
_____
_____
_____
_____
_____
_____

DAY 15
THE HARDEST PART

The hard truth

By now you've likely identified what the hardest part is for you. The thing you find most unbearable about the loss of your companion.

Maybe it's your morning routine without them. Or the empty spot on your bed where they used to sleep. Or the eerie silence in your home. Or the way they used to sit on your lap. Or their purr. Or their bark. Or their song. Or their…presence.

There's always something we miss the most that makes the loss that much harder to get over and move on from. For me, it's the feeling of draping my cat over my shoulder, where he would live for as long as I'd let him stay, purring loudly and triumphantly.

Sometimes I find myself imagining him there. I think of his smell, the fluffiness of his fur around my neck, and the feeling of his purr vibrating through my body. I miss him terribly, but in certain moments, this visualization actually soothes me.

The silver lining

There's bound to be a thing you find the most difficult about your loss. Recognize that this is important so you can help yourself work through those tough moments. Once you identify and come to terms with it, you can make an effort to create new routines and habits to fill the void.

"It takes strength to make your way through grief, to grab hold of life and let it pull you forward."

PATTI DAVIS

JOURNALING TIME

What's the hardest part about dealing with the loss of your companion? Why?

_____
_____
_____
_____
_____
_____
_____

What are some ideas you have about how you can reframe this difficult situation so it's less painful and more joyful moving forward?

_____
_____
_____
_____
_____
_____
_____

DAY 16
COPING WITH LONELINESS

The hard truth

When our pet leaves us, there's a massive void. Life feels empty and lonely. Even if you have a full family, children at home and another surviving pet, it's not the same. Your lost companion brought their own energy and personality to everyone's life. And now they are sorely missed and you feel lonely.

I feel the loneliest during my nighttime work sessions. Ever since my children were babies, I've worked at night. Originally, I did this because I had to. It was the way I kept my business running while also giving myself to my children during the day. I always thought eventually, I'd give up that nighttime session but over the years, I've come to embrace it. The house is quiet and I suppose I'm a bit of a night owl. Over the last several years, for some reason, I moved my nighttime work session out of my office and over to the family room on the couch with my laptop. And who was always there with me from start to finish? My Hanky.

Now, I still have my nighttime work sessions on the sofa but they are far lonelier than they were before. I am so grateful to have my other cat, Roxy, still with me and that intelligent and intuitive creature now snuggles on my lap or against my legs as I work. But the edge of the couch is still empty. Even though I'm not alone, I'm still lonely.

The greatest gift our pets give us is companionship. I remember despising the feeling of being home alone in my early adulthood. That is, until we adopted two kittens. I never minded again, and would relish the quiet time with the companionship of my felines.

When our pets leave us, they take their companionship with them. Sure, we can remember them and think of them and hold them dearly in our hearts, but that doesn't bring them back to us. It doesn't let us feel their warmth and company.

The silver lining

I'm not going to tell you you'll stop missing your pet one day soon. You may not; you may never. What I *am* going to tell you is that loneliness can be tolerated and dealt with effectively. Surround yourself with loved ones as much as possible. Give your other pet(s) tons of love and attention. Read a heartwarming book. Journal about your feelings. Watch a funny movie. Keep yourself busy. Meet up with friends. Be with family.

Over time, your loneliness will dissipate, and perhaps far faster, if you are open to giving a home to another little companion.

"Loneliness is the shadow that brightens the light of the soul."

UNKNOWN SOURCE

JOURNALING TIME

When do you feel the loneliest? Why?

_____
_____
_____
_____
_____
_____
_____

Write down a few things you think might help you feel less lonely.

_____
_____
_____
_____
_____
_____
_____
_____
_____

DAY 17
SIGNS AND SYMBOLS

The hard truth

You feel the presence of your pet after they're gone. Crazy? Not exactly...

One of my friends said to me recently, "Your cat is still with you in your home. Cats love their spots."

If you believe in the slightest possibility of something beyond the physical world where we find ourselves now, then perhaps our pets do stay with us for some time after they pass.

Have you ever experienced a moment where you thought you saw them? Perhaps walking past your room or a fleeting movement out of the corner of your eye. You may have shrugged this off as nothing more than your mind playing tricks on you, but maybe it was more than that.

Many pet owners believe their deceased companions pay regular visits after they're gone. Sometimes these encounters come in the form of the subtle sound of their paws on the stairs, a sudden bark out of nowhere, the sensation of them brushing past a leg or the appearance of a dip at the corner of the bed where they once lay.

The silver lining

There is much we don't know for certain in our lives. Gut instinct goes a long way in such scenarios. If you believe you are feeling the presence of your pet who's passed, you may indeed be right. While you'll never know if their visit was real, one thing is for sure: you're in good company with your belief.

"Perhaps they are not stars in the sky, but rather openings where our loved ones shine down to let us know they are happy."

INUIT PROVERB

JOURNALING TIME

Have you received any signs or signals from your pet? What makes you think they're still with you, or paying little visits every now and then?

_____
_____
_____
_____
_____
_____

How does their presence make you feel?

_____
_____
_____
_____
_____
_____

DAY 18
WHAT YOUR PET TAUGHT YOU

The hard truth

I believe every pet teaches us something. They come into our lives for a reason. When it's really meant to be and the fit is just right, the most suitable pet chooses you just as much as you choose them.

It's not always easy to identify their teachings while they're still living. Life can get busy and chaotic and how often do we really find ourselves stopping to reflect on what our pet is teaching us along the way? But when we find a moment to be still and to think about the journey we've shared, there's always a lesson that stands tall, like a single flower among the weeds.

Betty showed me what true feline companionship was, day in and day out as she followed me around and always told me what was on her mind. Hank taught me to slow down. To stop and just *be* for a few minutes each day. To take a bit of time with him, before rushing off to work. He taught me about the importance of bringing a little calm into my life.

The silver lining

Whatever you believe your pet was here to teach you, write it down. Remember it. Make an effort to practice it and incorporate it into your daily life. If you can, and if you make a point of doing it, this is the best way to ensure that your beloved pet lives on forever.

"Those who teach us the most about humanity aren't always humans."

UNKNOWN SOURCE

JOURNALING TIME

What did your pet teach you?

_____
_____
_____
_____
_____
_____
_____

How can you carry those lessons forward into your life?

_____
_____
_____
_____
_____
_____
_____

DAY 19
SHIFTING FOCUS

The hard truth

When we're grieving, we want to stay in it – at least for a little while. Grief drags us down and pulls us into a darker place than we're used to. Unlike other adverse scenarios we can't wait to get over and get out of, the odd part about grief is that it can make you want it. It can make you want the pain and suffering that defines it. And this is because grief requires time. It *needs* time. You can't rush it or get away from it. Grief will find you. Over and over again, it will come back. Until you give it *time*. To process and to run its course.

At some point, however, it'll be time to switch your focus. The next phase will arrive in which you begin to let go of your sadness and sorrows just a little, to welcome new feelings. These will be feelings of appreciation, gratitude and happiness for all that you shared with your special companion while they were here. There's no need to force it; trust that you'll know when the time is right.

Up until this point, your mind has probably been almost solely inundated with the haunting memories of your pet as they passed. It's a difficult image to shake off, but now is when you can try to see it in a new light – one that depicts your companion at peace, free from pain and onto their next beautiful version of life.

The silver lining

When you reframe your perception, you change your mood and general outlook. Focus on the fact that your pet is happy now, smiling down on you (or maybe right at you from the sofa over there). Instead of focusing on the end, cast your mind back to months or years ago when they were their best selves. *This* is the image to remember and to cherish forever.

"Death leaves a heartache no one can heal, love leaves a memory no one can steal."

IRISH HEADSTONE

JOURNALING TIME

Do you feel ready and willing to shift your focus? Why or why not?

_____
_____
_____
_____
_____
_____

Describe one memory of your pet in their prime that sticks in your head.

_____
_____
_____
_____
_____
_____
_____
_____

DAY 20
ADAPTING

The hard truth

Adapting is difficult. We become set in our ways, in our daily routines and in the characteristics that make up our lives. When something happens that disrupts our familiarities and reforms our reality, we are forced to adapt. There's just one problem: we don't want to.

As much as we may be reluctant to adapt at first, human beings are innately adaptable. As Charles Darwin once said, "It is not the strongest of the species that survives, nor the most intelligent. It is the one that is the most adaptable to change." And that's exactly how human beings have been able to survive and thrive for so many centuries.

In the case of your lost pet, unfortunately, you don't have much of a choice. There's nothing you can do about their passing and you have zero control over the situation. You can't bring them back; their time had come. When you find it within yourself to accept this, there is only one way forward: adapt to life without them in it.

The silver lining

Adaptation is your key to thriving, even without your pet.

It starts with a shift from remorse and anger, to peace and gratitude. Your vision will become less clouded by sadness and intense emotions and you'll begin to see the situation a little differently. You'll be ready and willing to remember what a great life you gave your pet and what incredible memories you made together. Each new day that arrives, you'll carry this strong feeling of gratitude with you and you'll visualize your pet in a positive, happy light.

You *will* adapt to life without your companion. You'll see.

"My mind still talks to you and my heart still looks for you, but my soul knows you are at peace."

UNKNOWN SOURCE

JOURNALING TIME

Have you started to adapt to the loss of your pet? If yes, describe how. If no, what ideas do you have about how you might be able to begin?

_____
_____
_____
_____
_____
_____
_____
_____
_____
_____
_____
_____
_____
_____

DAY 21
PROGRESS

The hard truth

Progress takes time and effort. Sometimes it's slow and other times it's fast. When it comes to grief, you can't rush progress. It's one of those things that happens in its own time.

This is not to say that your grief ever ends. In a way, it stays with us forever, as does the cherished memory of your companion. You'll never forget and you'll never stop missing them, you'll simply find a way to progress and move on.

One day, you'll find yourself thinking of your pet and you won't burst into tears. Someone will bring their name up and you'll be able to share a story without breaking down. Or you'll have a moment where you see an old picture of them and a smile forms upon your face.

That's progress.

Every little bit of progress you notice during this tough time must be acknowledged and celebrated. Take note of your positive changes and give yourself credit where it's due. Remind yourself that it *is* getting better. Slowly but surely, you're healing. And that's a beautiful thing.

The silver lining

Progress is inevitable. Time is your best friend right now and with every moment that passes, even though it represents yet another minute you're forced to live without your pet, it's also a minute that makes you that much more comfortable in your new situation.

You're progressing and everything is going to be alright.

"The reality is that you will grieve forever. You will not 'get over' the loss of a loved one; you'll learn to live with it. You will heal and you will rebuild yourself around the loss you have suffered. You will be whole again but you will never be the same. Nor should you be the same, nor would you want to."

ELISABETH KÜBLER-ROSS & DAVID KESSLER

JOURNALING TIME

What little progresses have you made so far?

_____
_____
_____
_____
_____
_____
_____
_____

How do these mini advancements make you feel?

_____
_____
_____
_____

DAY 22
THE DAY WE MET

The hard truth

This memory is tender. But it's also incredible. It marks the day that your journey together began. The same way you're without your pet now, so you were every moment before this day, too.

If you're a pet lover, they come and go all through your life. Some stay for long periods and some only a short little while. The important part is that you make the most of the time you have.

As you cast your mind back to the day you first locked eyes with your companion, take a few minutes to reflect on the experience. Think about where you were, what the place looked like, the smell that filled your nostrils, which way you walked to meet them, the exact point where you saw them, the feeling of first contact and connection, and finally, the second when you knew they were the one.

Hank was at a large shelter. Oddly enough, we heard about him from the family who adopted our previous insane, Jekyll-Hyde cat because their daughter worked there. To this day, I have no idea why they didn't adopt Hank themselves! And I am eternally grateful for their decision. We walked in and almost instantly saw a gorgeous orange tabby standing with paws on the window to our left. I said, "I bet that's Hank." And it was. We went into the room and my husband hoisted him up to his shoulder, where he happily stayed for a long time, purring like a motorboat. The rest is history.

The silver lining

There will only ever be one perfect first day, but you have (hopefully) years' worth of memories, all thanks to that magical moment when your paths crossed exactly how they needed to.

"What's meant to be will always find a way."

UNKNOWN SOURCE

JOURNALING TIME

How did you meet your pet? Describe the day. Pretend you're writing a scene in a movie to make the memory vivid. (Think about the five senses: sight, sound, smell, touch and taste.)

DAY 23
DREAMING OF THEM

The hard truth

Dreams can be so vivid, so real. They can pound us right back to painful moments we've experienced, or catapult us into joyful fairytale-like visions. A powerful dream can make us wake up in a sweat feeling stressed, or with peace in our heart and a smile on our face.

When an event in our life becomes top of mind, chances are we may find ourselves dreaming about it. Dreams about your pet may come in the form of still photos, fleeting images or passive movements, where nothing really happens and your pet is simply with you as you sleep. Others may represent an event that takes place, which could be based on a memory or a fictitious story. And sometimes, your pet may come to you in a visitation dream.

Many people have reported dreams about their pets following their death, and visitation dreams in particular, in which the pet appears happy, healthy and full of life, there to deliver some kind of message to the dreamer. Lovingly and telepathically, deceased pets have been reported to make their owners feel calm, less sad and deeply loved through profound dream experiences.

The silver lining

If you so choose, dreams about your pet can be thought of as the medium through which their presence is still with you. You're dreaming about them because you miss them deeply and you're grieving, and when they appear, it's their way of telling you they're okay now. They've moved on to their next chapter, and you don't need to feel sad anymore. You'll meet again one day.

"Feathers that flutter, fur that gleams, the essence of you in our dreams. A presence felt in the quiet night, a guardian spirit, pure and bright."

UNKNOWN SOURCE

JOURNALING TIME

Describe any dreams you've had about your pet and how you felt when you woke up.

DAY 24
A TRIBUTE TO YOUR PET'S LIFE

The hard truth

Even though it might hurt, paying tribute to your pet's life can work wonders for your healing process. Celebrating any life that has been lived involves honoring something that's no longer with us. When you commemorate your pet, you allow yourself to let go – just a little. Instead of focusing on your anger, shock, sadness or reluctance, you *accept*. You come to terms with the fact that they're gone and while you know you'll miss them forever, you thank your lucky stars that your paths crossed.

Unlike when a person passes away, there are no hard-pressed societal norms and pressures to which we feel the need to abide when a pet leaves this world. Paying tribute to their life can be anything, from a grand event to a small gesture. Bury your pet and have a ceremony. Host a memorial service with extended family. Write a story about your pet's life. Journal about special moments you shared. Draw a picture. Frame a photo.

My children tattooed all of our arms with markers. They drew hearts, portraits of Hank and his name. It was so sweet. Then they proceeded to print their favorite photos and create collages of him on their bulletin boards. Since that day, they've also changed the backgrounds on their iPads to Hanky photos, too. My mom is a glass artist and even she paid tribute by creating a gorgeous glass piece of art with Hank and Roxy sitting in a tree facing the night sky. And me? My biggest tribute is this very journal.

Thank you, Hank.

The silver lining

Paying tribute to your pet's life signifies a profound step forward in your grieving process. Be proud of yourself for coming this far and feel good about the fact that you've honored the life of your pet with care, love and a whole lot of tears.

"Like a bird singing in the rain,
let grateful memories survive in
times of sorrow."

ROBERT LOUIS STEVENSON

JOURNALING TIME

Have you paid tribute to your pet's life yet? If yes, how? If no, what ideas come to mind about how you can celebrate them and accept your loss?

_____
_____
_____
_____
_____
_____

How do you feel after?

_____
_____
_____
_____

DAY 25
FINDING COMFORT

The hard truth

Some days, comfort is easy to find. A friend who reaches out. A phone call from Mom. Hugs from your spouse. Laughter with your kids. A good book and a cozy blanket. Other days, it's far more difficult and all you can do is sit in your lonesomeness and let the tears flow.

Even though some time has passed, your grief is still like the ocean waves. There are highs and lows, comfort and discomfort. Whichever part of the wave you're riding, keep your head up and watch the sandy shore just ahead. You'll meet the steadiness of land soon enough.

In the meantime, seek out comfort and don't be afraid to ask for it. Whatever you need is fine; whatever you need is good. Eat the tub of ice cream. Take your kids to the mall. Watch a movie with your partner. Snuggle and smother your existing pet. Talk to your lost pet. Cry to your friend on the phone. Pay tribute. Remember. Forget. Take a break.

The silver lining

Take comfort in the fact that even when you feel down and out, when your grief swirls around you like a tornado and when you don't have the strength to push through, it will pass. Those intense feelings will fizzle. The downward wave will indeed travel upward again. This is the cycle of grief; it's the cycle of life.

"Deep grief is almost like a specific location, a coordinate on a map of time. When you are standing in that forest of sorrow, you cannot imagine that you could ever find your way to a better place. But if someone can assure you that they themselves have stood in that same place, and have now moved on, sometimes this will bring hope."

ELIZABETH GILBERT

JOURNALING TIME

Make a list of everything that brings you comfort right now.

_____
_____
_____
_____
_____
_____

Think of one comforting thing you can fit in each day this week.

_____
_____
_____
_____
_____
_____

DAY 26
THE LOVE THAT REMAINS

The hard truth

Love is there. It always was and it always will be. When we lose a pet who we've loved so deeply, the grief we experience is that much more intense. This causes an inevitable question to pop into our heads: *Was it all worth it?*

Only you can answer this but in my experience the answer is always the same: *Yes. A thousand times over, yes.* To have had the presence and company of your pet for a while; to have had the pleasure of befriending them and building unbreakable trust; to have created a one-of-a-kind bond; to have held them close; to have snuggled on a countless number of occasions; to have cared for them and they for you…

This is what love is. And this is the kind of love that remains – irrespective of separation, illness or death. It's a love that lives on no matter what. The hard part is that because it's so strong and because it survives everything, it hurts. Sometimes it actually feels painful to love in such a way and to feel it long after the passing of your companion.

The silver lining

You know the well-known saying by Alfred Lord Tennyson, "'Tis better to have loved and lost than never to have loved at all." Of course, this discounts the days and weeks immediately following a big loss but what I invite you to see and remember is the beauty and purity in the love you shared with your pet. Nothing can break it. And that isn't a bad thing; it's an incredible thing.

All that love which remains lives on for your pet, for you, and since there's so much of it, maybe, just maybe, for another.

"It is the most unselfish act in
all of life to let one go that we
have found beloved."

KATIE MCGAHAN

JOURNALING TIME

Do you still feel a strong love for your pet? Describe it.

_____
_____
_____
_____
_____
_____
_____

Do you believe this love will remain forever? Why or why not?

_____
_____
_____
_____
_____
_____
_____

DAY 27
WARMING UP TO THE IDEA OF ANOTHER

The hard truth

Figuring out the right time to start thinking about and pursuing the possibility of a new pet feels impossible! That's because there is no right time. There are no rules you need to follow or timeframes you must satisfy.

For some, a significant mourning time is essential. They cannot wrap their heads around the idea of another pet too soon. Waiting, processing and healing take priority. For others, the sooner the better to welcome a new companion into their homes because they need somewhere to put all that love. Taking on a new pet is inevitable in their minds, so then, they decide there's no point in waiting. Bringing in another helps to ease the pain and distract the mind. And in the latter case, the grieving process happens simultaneously. After all, just because you have a new pet doesn't mean you don't mourn the last.

Perhaps *you* are considering the possibility of adopting or rescuing another animal. There's no need to feel guilty or bad about it. You're not replacing your lost companion – they are irreplaceable. Whether it happens quickly or slowly, that's up to you and your family. If and when you decide the time is right, remember that you're doing an amazing deed by giving a warm, cozy and wonderful home to another pet who needs one.

The silver lining

A new pet might just be the thing you need most in your life right now – or days, weeks, months down the road. Every animal is unique and special, and getting to know another will only further enrich your life in ways you cannot begin to understand until you do it.

"A new dog never replaces an old dog, it merely expands the heart. If you have loved many dogs your heart is very big."

ERICA JONG

JOURNALING TIME

Do you feel ready to explore the possibility of getting a new pet? Why or why not?

_____
_____
_____
_____
_____
_____
_____
_____
_____
_____
_____
_____
_____

DAY 28
FOREVER IN YOUR HEART

The hard truth

As more days pass, it may surprise you how many times your pet continues to pop into your mind. Some days, you'll feel great and you'll be confident that you're turning a corner. And then all of a sudden, your wave comes crashing downwards again and you feel like you're right back where you started. This is because your pet is *forever in your heart*.

Losing a beloved pet never truly stops hurting. Time may soften the sharp edges of grief, but the space they filled in your heart will always be theirs. Some days, you'll inevitably find yourself longing to hear their paws on the floor, feel their warmth beside you or see their eyes full of love. No matter how much healing happens, their absence will always be felt.

The silver lining

While they're no longer physically by your side, they'll always be a part of you. The love you shared doesn't vanish—it lives on in your memories, in the lessons they taught you and in the way they changed your heart. Every time you speak their name, smile at a memory or feel their presence in quiet moments, they are still with you. Love like that never fades; it simply transforms.

Deep within you, in the pit of your chest, where your heart beats on and on with the methodic pumping of life, that's where your pet resides.

"I loved you your whole life and I'll miss you the rest of mine."

UNKNOWN SOURCE

JOURNALING TIME

Is your grieving process getting easier? How?

_____
_____
_____
_____
_____
_____
_____

What is it about your pet that you know will stay in your heart forever?

_____
_____
_____
_____
_____

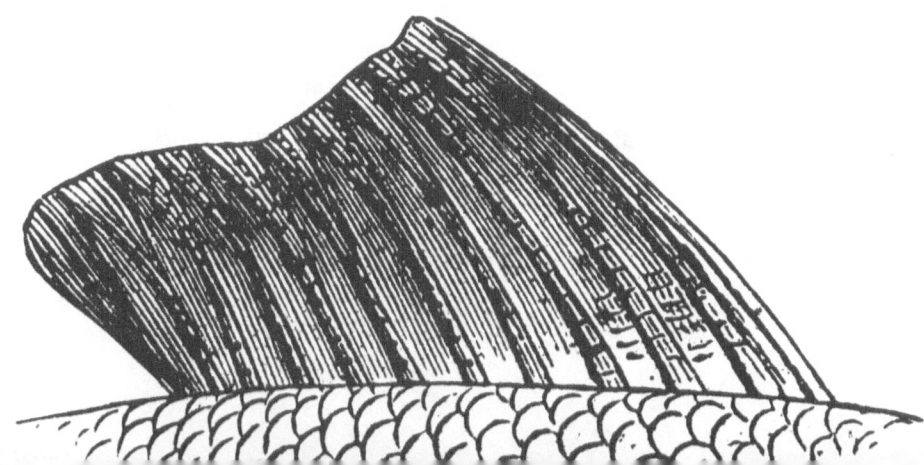

DAY 29
FINDING PEACE

The hard truth

Peace may not come all at once. It may not come at all for a while. Instead of thinking about peace as the be-all-end-all final state of your grieving process, consider it in bits and pieces. One morning you may wake up feeling quite peaceful and accepting of your loss. That very same afternoon, all the peace might wash away, leaving you in a rotten and sullen state. Be prepared for your peace to come and go.

As you struggle and search for peace in your life without your companion, I have found it particularly helpful to remind myself of a few important things:

1. We shared a significant amount of time together.
2. We gave him an incredible home filled with love.
3. He gave us unconditional love and company.
4. There were lots of beautiful moments.

5. My pet knew how much I loved him and I know how much he loved me.
6. I was there for him when he needed me.
7. I gave him the best possible care.
8. In the end, his body decided its time here was up (I think his mind and soul were content in staying).
9. He couldn't last forever.
10. But in my heart, he will.

The silver lining

It's time for you to find peace in the fact that there was nothing more you could have done. No matter what the impossible circumstance, your pet's passing was meant to be. It was their time. Relinquish all feelings of control and resistance.

Give in to what *is* and make the most of it.

"I've found that there is always some beauty left – in nature, sunshine, freedom, in yourself; these can all help you."

ANNE FRANK

JOURNALING TIME

If you wanted yourself to find peace in the loss of your pet, what would you say?

_____
_____
_____
_____
_____
_____
_____
_____
_____
_____
_____

DAY 30
BEING HAPPY

The hard truth

There's no hard truth in being happy. Happiness is a wonderful thing and it's what we all strive for. It's the single most universal goal among human beings.

Wherever we live, whatever we have, whoever we are, we all want to be... HAPPY.

So, do it. Happiness is a choice. It's not something that happens *to* you; it's something you *create*. You have the power to mold and shape a life that invites and nourishes genuine happiness.

Start from the inside. Process your feelings. Recognize and understand your emotions. Communicate. Write. Draw. Then move to the outside. Carve out time for yourself and the things that matter to you. Clean your living space. Be creative. Take up a hobby. Read. Laugh. And continue to love to the fullest.

Don't be afraid to love again. Your pet wants you to. Animal lovers are for life and when you open your heart time and time again, you expand your ability to love. And a life full of love is a rich life indeed.

The silver lining

Your happiness may be painted differently now. Today's canvas might not look the same as yesterday's. But it's there. Bright, colorful and alive as can be. It's up to you to pick up your paintbrush and make a new stroke on your canvas. Your work isn't done.

Every great composition is always in progress. It's never finished. It merely represents a point in time when the paintbrush was set down, when the fingers left the keys, when the pencil was laid on the table. Maybe to start a new piece. Maybe to take a break. Maybe to let in something new.

You *can* be happy.

So, be happy.

"I was a light in your life when
I was alive. Let me continue to
be a light on your path
through life now that I have
passed."

YOUR ANGEL PET

JOURNALING TIME

Describe how you feel when you are genuinely happy.

_____
_____
_____
_____
_____
_____

Tell your pet how they made you happy when they were here, and how you plan to carry that happiness forward, even though they're gone.

_____
_____
_____
_____
_____
_____

THANK YOU

Thank you for walking through this grief journey with me. From my heart to yours, I wish you well, fellow pet owner. If this journal helped you in any way, please leave me a review. Each one helps tremendously and I would be so grateful.

I have a FREE GIFT for you! It's something that I hope will touch your heart the way it did mine. Scan this QR code to claim it now!

www.ingramcontent.com/pod-product-compliance
Lightning Source LLC
Chambersburg PA
CBHW030336010526
44119CB00047B/515